What Is the Book About?

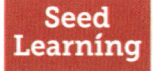

princess

witch

dragon

hero

pirate

king

fairy

monster

What is the book about?

It's about a hero.

What is the book about?

It's about a dragon.

What is the book about?

It's about a monster.

Let's learn about Laos.

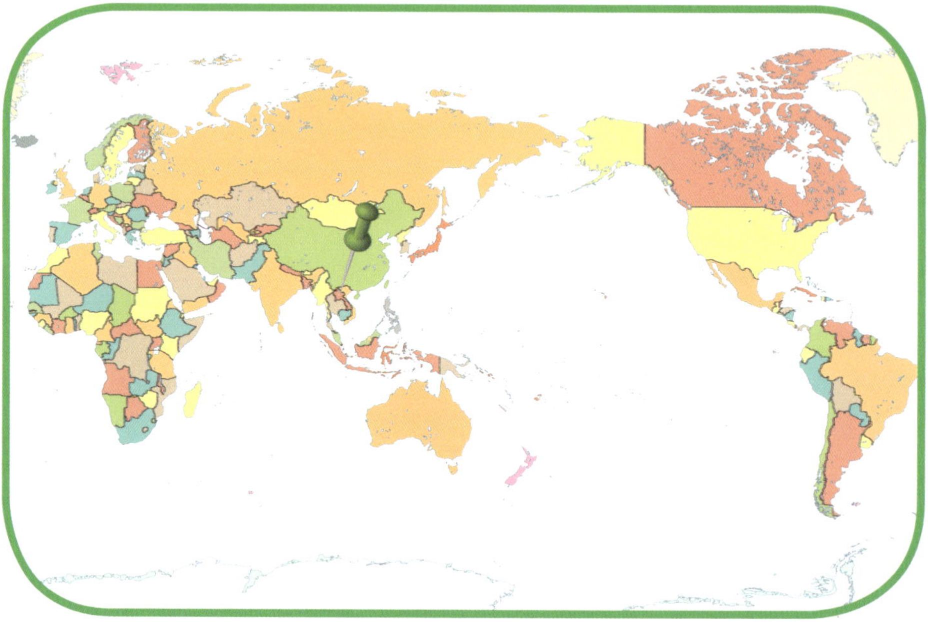

Flag of Laos

Pha That Luang
Temple